DATE DUE

FEB.19.2000			
JUL.11.2000			

Demco, Inc. 38-293

EXTREME MACHINES
UNDER THE SEA

PATRICIA ARMENTROUT

The Rourke Press, Inc.
Vero Beach, Florida 32964

Patricia Armentrout specializes in nonfiction writing and has had several book series published for primary schools. She resides in Cincinnati with her husband and two children.

PHOTO CREDITS:
© Corel Corporation: page 13; © Defense Visual Information Center: pages 12, 16; © Harbor Branch Oceanographic Institution Inc., Ft. Pierce, FL: cover; © International Stock: page 4; © Kogler Corp./Intl. Stock: page 7; © Naval Historical Foundation Photo Service: page 9; © NOAA: pages 6, 18, 21; © Keith Wood/Intl. Stock: page 15; © Woods Hole Oceanographic Institution: pages 10, 19; © UNCW/NOAA National Undersea Research Center: page 22

EDITORIAL SERVICES:
Penworthy Learning Systems

Library of Congress Cataloging-in-Publication Data

Armentrout, Patricia, 1960-
   Extreme machines under the sea / Patricia Armentrout.
     p. cm. — (Extreme machines)
   Includes index.
   Summary: Describes different kinds of submersibles, ships that can go underwater, including submarines, bathyscaphes, and the ABE or Autonomous Benthic Explorer.
   ISBN 1-57103-213-4
   1. Submarines (Ships)—Juvenile literature. [1. Submarines. 2. Submarine boats.] I. Armentrout, Patricia. 1960- II. Title III. Series: Extreme machines.
VM365.A76 1998
623.8'205—dc21
                                              98–24065
                                               CIP
                                               AC

Printed in the USA

TABLE OF CONTENTS

UNDER THE SEA

Exploring the deep blue sea: Many people dream of it, but very few have actually done it. Why are people so interested with what is below the ocean surface? People study the ocean depths to learn about the past and to see what the future may bring.

It takes special equipment and machines to explore underwater. This book will look at machines used under the sea.

A nuclear submarine is an extreme undersea machine that can travel below or on the ocean surface.

SUBMERSIBLE

A **submersible** (sub MER suh bul) is a ship that can go underwater. Small submersibles are hauled on bigger ships and then lowered into the water when ready to be used.

The submersible Pisces returns to its mother ship.

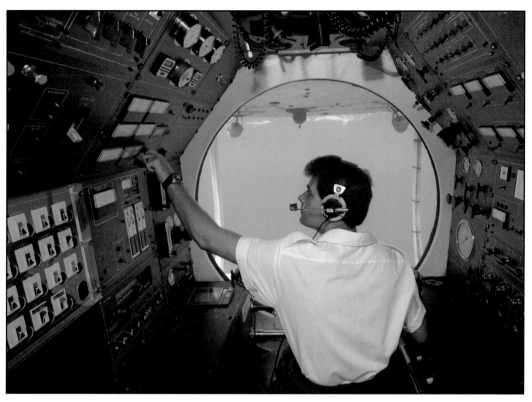

This submarine has a window for viewing undersea life.

Submersibles are used for many reasons: Some help people locate shipwrecks or lost equipment; others are used in underwater construction.

Jacques Cousteau, probably the most famous underwater explorer, used his Diving Saucer submersible to study undersea plants and animals.

BATHYSCAPHE

A **bathyscaphe** (BATH i SKAF) is a submersible made for deep sea exploration. Bathyscaphes are small and hold only two or three people. They have a lot of equipment inside and special cameras and lights on the outside.

In 1960 the bathyscaphe Trieste took a two-man crew down 35,800 feet (10,912 meters) below the surface. The men sat in a gorge, called Challenger Deep, in the Pacific Ocean south of Japan.

The two men and Trieste set a world record for reaching the deepest known point on Earth. Without the bathyscaphe the men would not have survived the water pressure at that depth.

The Historic Trieste holds the record for the world's deepest undersea dive.

ABE

ABE stands for **autonomous benthic explorer**
(aw TAHN uh mus) (BEN thik) (ik SPLAWR er).
ABE is an undersea exploring machine. ABE is
about 10 feet (3.05 meters) long and has seven
thrusters that move it through the water. While
underwater, it collects information from the sea
floor using cameras.

ABE is not always on the move. A computer
works as ABE's brain and tells ABE when to
work and when to "sleep." ABE sits on the ocean
floor when sleeping—saving energy. ABE can go
on short day trips or stay underwater up to a year.

*ABE is an underwater robot that can explore areas too dangerous for
manned submersibles.*

SUBMARINE

A submarine is a submersible made of inner and outer steel shells. Between the shells are tanks. When the tanks are filled with seawater, the ship can dive. The ship will rise, or surface, when **compressed air** (kum PREST AIR) is forced into the tanks, removing the water.

Crew members inspect the attack submarine USS Pargo after it surfaced through the ice.

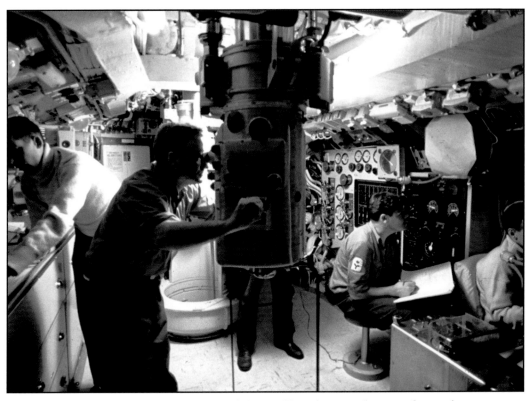
Special equipment lines the inside walls of a nuclear submarine.

Many naval submarines are **nuclear powered** (NOO klee ur POW erd). A nuclear reactor produces steam that propels the engines. Nuclear power also provides electricity to run all the equipment on the sub.

Nuclear-powered subs need not surface except to board supplies or change crew members—which usually happens every few months.

OFF-SHORE OIL RIG

Where does oil come from? Much of the world's oil supply is found deep below the ocean floor. Off-shore drilling rigs are used to find and recover the oil.

Off-shore oil drilling rigs have giant platforms with strong legs that are anchored to the ocean floor. Some oil rigs are big enough for their crews to live and work on for months at a time.

To recover the oil, a steel bit, or drill, is attached to a drill pipe and lowered to the sea floor. The bit turns and cuts into the ocean floor. When the drill pipe reaches the oil, the oil is pumped to the surface and stored in huge tanks.

This oil production platform towers above the waters of the Gulf of Mexico.

DSRV

Unfortunately submarine disasters do happen. In 1963, the nuclear sub Thresher submerged and never returned to the surface. Over a hundred lives were lost. The U.S. Navy now uses a rescue submersible called a deep submergence rescue vehicle, or **DSRV**.

A submarine carries the small rescue sub to the disabled submarine. When launched, the rescue sub attaches to the sunken submarine's rescue hatch. The DSRV will carry up to 24 people and can return to the sunken sub as many times as needed.

A small rescue sub is carried on the back of a nuclear attack submarine.

ALVIN AND JASON

Alvin, designed and named by Alyn Vine, is one of the most famous deep sea exploring machines. It has gone on many important underwater journeys.

Alvin completes 150-200 ocean dives every year.

Jason is a robot that is controlled by a team of scientists working on the surface.

In 1986, Alvin and its crew of three went down 13,000 feet (3,962 meters) in the icy North Atlantic waters. The crew used special equipment to photograph the Titanic wreck.

Unmanned submersibles are also used to explore underwater. Jason Jr., a remote-controlled vehicle, explored the Titanic wreck in more detail.

UNDERWATER HABITAT

An underwater **habitat** (HAB i tat) is a workstation. It stays underwater for days or even weeks at a time. People who live in these habitats are called **aquanauts** (AK wuh NAWTS).

A habitat's air pressure equals the water pressure around it. The habitat is full of equipment that helps aquanauts conduct experiments, collect samples, and send results to a workstation on the surface.

Habitats allow scientists to explore the ocean for long periods without needing to surface.

The Aquarius habitat allows aquanauts to live and work underwater for long periods of time.

GLOSSARY

autonomous benthic explorer (aw TAHN uh mus) (BEN thik) (ik SPLAWR er) — a self-moving machine that collects information from the ocean floor

aquanauts (AK wuh NAWTS) — underwater divers who live and work inside an underwater shelter

bathyscaphe (BATH i SKAF) — a submersible ship used for deep-sea exploration

compressed air (kum PREST AIR) — air under pressure inside a container

DSRV (Deep Submergence Rescue Vehicle) — a small submersible used to rescue people from sunken submarines

habitat (HAB i tat) — a shelter designed for long stays underwater

nuclear powered (NOO klee ur POW erd) — powered by the energy released when tiny bits, called atoms, are split

submersible (sub MER suh bul) — watercraft that travels underwater

An aquanaut inspects the condition of the underwater habitat Aquarius.

INDEX

FURTHER READING

Find out more about Extreme Machines with these helpful books:
Jensen, Dr. Anthony; and Bolt, Dr. Stephen. *Undersea Mission.* Gareth Stevens Children's Books, 1989.
Rutland, J. *See Inside a Submarine.* Warwick Press, 1988.